Here is a new collection of exciting puzzles, word games and exercises—all based entirely on Scripture. Now you can bring the whole family together for hours of fun-filled activity while you test each member's biblical knowledge. MORE BIBLE PUZZLES AND GAMES provides questions **and answers** which vary in difficulty and are equally suitable for beginning as well as advanced students of the Bible. Discover learning fun and valuable lesson guides for you and everyone you know.

BY M. J. Capley

Bible Puzzle and Game Book
More Bible Puzzles and Games

More Bible Puzzles and Games

M. J. CAPLEY

SPIRE BOOKS

Fleming H. Revell Company
Old Tappan, New Jersey

All quotations used in this volume are based on the King James Version of the Bible.

Library of Congress Cataloging in Publication Data

Capley, MJ
More Bible puzzles and games.

(Spire books)
1. Bible games and puzzles. I. Title.
GV1507.B5C36 207 78-9151
ISBN 0-8007-8320-4

A Spire Book

Published by Fleming H. Revell Company

Printed in the United States of America
This is an original Spire book,
published by Spire Books,
a Division of Fleming H. Revell Company,
Old Tappan, New Jersey

Contents

More Bible Puzzles and Games

Riddles—1

Guess who these people are.

1. This king did not smoke grass; he ate it.
2. He had a whale of a story to tell.
3. This couple ate themselves to death.
4. He was held up during a battle.
5. He discovered that there was money in fish.
6. She got carried away just like her husband.
7. She never became ruthless, even though she lost both her sons.
8. This person had a hidden talent.
9. He had a salty wife.
10. Why didn't Cain raise sheep?

Riddles—2

Guess who these people are.

1. He really lost his head because of a woman.
2. He certainly was not the Wizard of Uz.
3. He was never guilty of being late because he was an early man.
4. People weren't joking when they called her a witch.
5. She was an aqueous artist in the Book of Exodus.
6. This man was speechless when he heard that his wife would bear him a son.
7. He used a foxy method to destroy the crops of the Philistines.
8. He broke all the Ten Commandments at one time.
9. This ghost does not haunt houses.
10. She gave with all her mite.

Riddles—3

Guess who or what these are.

1. In which season did man first commit sin?
2. He was a statuesque dreamer.
3. This boy observed sheep, and he later moved on to greater subjects.
4. This ladder was not used for home repairs.
5. David could have called him a giant of a man.
6. One could say that he saw the light and changed his ways.
7. This bread was really flat.
8. Joab realized that this man's hang-up was a tree.
9. Even though he was a deacon, this man got stoned.
10. From his name, one might think that he flew an airplane.

Riddles—4

Guess who these people are.

1. Pharaoh's favorite ruler didn't measure inches.
2. He was not robbed, but he was held up by water.
3. No one could accuse this king of being hartless.
4. He never had to sell himself before others because his brothers did it for him.
5. She added a bit of spice to Christ's life in the house of Simon the leper.
6. Jesus and Martha both saw him return from a grave situation.
7. He was not poor, but he rent his clothes because of Joseph.
8. Elisha could have called him a "little dipper."
9. He was not a cook, but he wore an apron just the same.
10. David could have called him a compulsive lier.

Riddles—5

Guess who or what these are.

1. His subjects could have said to him, "Don't be such a wise guy!"
2. How were Pharaoh's horses like artists?
3. He was not a loser, but he was still licked.
4. It is a book that contains sixty-six books.
5. He heard it straight from the ass's mouth.
6. One could call it a floating zoo.
7. He might have enjoyed a spare rib.
8. She was dying to touch Christ.
9. How did Paul treat the people of the church at Ephesus like envelopes?
10. She raised Cain in her day.

Hidden Women

Underline the names of women hidden in the sentences below. The woman in the first sentence has already been underlined.

1. Asa, Raham, and Ezbon are men who can be found in the Bible.
2. Sin can mar your testimony.
3. Adam walked thru the garden.
4. The veil was worn by women for concealment.
5. Belshazzar indulged in a great feast while a hand wrote upon the wall.
6. Can you tell me in which era Chelubai lived?
7. Pride can mar that inner communion with God.
8. Ah, a garden is a lovely place in which to pray.
9. How many places thereabouts did Paul visit?
10. Other than Nahum, were there any prophets of Judah?

Hidden Men

Underline the names of men hidden in the sentences below. The man in the first sentence has already been underlined.

1. He finally learned to set hate aside.
2. Melissa ultimately asked for forgiveness.
3. Kate said, "I will watch my step henceforth."
4. Even tho' *master* had various meanings, Christ was addressed as "Master."
5. Jessica invited me to church next Sunday.
6. Ann finally accepted Christ as her Saviour.
7. God can deliver us from all evil.
8. I know that he's austere in his beliefs.
9. A Christian is also known as a believer.
10. Jan said, "Papa ultimately became a preacher."

Hidden Diseases

Underline the diseases in the sentences below. The disease in the first sentence has already been underlined.

1. She thought that the Pharisees were a littl<u>e prosy</u>.
2. Usually a pal sympathizes with you.
3. They used a unit of dry measure known as cab.
4. He said, "I know about salvation; it changes your life."
5. Wicked kings sometimes staged foul ceremonies.
6. Abraham always displayed courtesy to a guest.
7. The rods of Moses and Aaron were supreme rods.
8. The Jews would not drop symbolism from their religious heritage.
9. The old man said, "Rub oil slowly into your wounds."
10. If every Christian would work harder, more people would be saved.

Hidden Numbers

Underline the numbers in the sentences below. The number in the first sentence has already been underlined.

1. The first woman was Eve.
2. Mother spoke of our dedication.
3. I am going to the rummage sale today, but Pat went yesterday.
4. The preacher's sermon was on eternal life.
5. Herodias, Eve, Naomi, and Leah were all mothers.
6. The old woman ate not of the fig tree.
7. Marsha asked, "If I verify your story, will you help me?"
8. Jim laughed, "You should have seen Bob's face when Beth reeled in that huge trout!"
9. Rachel, Eve, Naamah, and Miriam can all be found in the Old Testament.
10. Genesis records the curse of Cain in exile.

Hidden Books of the Bible

Underline the books of the Bible in the sentences below. The book of the Bible in the first sentence has already been underlined.

1. The old woman screamed, "<u>Tim, O, thy</u> healing was a miracle!"
2. Thebez, Rama, and Penuel are cities that can be found in the Bible.
3. An encampment of the Israelites near Mount Hor was called a Mosera.
4. Faith can wipe terror from one's brow.
5. Martha keeps alms for the poor.
6. She said, "I am at the Women's Bible League meeting."
7. One can study the tact so wonderfully exemplified by Jesus.
8. Terry shouted, "The answer is Ai. Aha, it's the city near the site of Abraham's first altar!"
9. Jud gestures frequently when he talks about Christ.
10. I have my Bible with me, but Gene's is in our car.

Hidden Parts of Man

Underline the parts of man in the sentences below. The first one has been underlined.

1. Be ye therefore as little children.
2. They, Sarah and Rebekah, were barren until God blessed them.
3. Anna, I like to study the Book of Genesis.
4. Abraham left his kin and moved away.
5. Did Paul ever go to Ephesus?
6. Humbly, she admitted her mistake.
7. We are in charge of organizing the new committee.
8. Sometimes there is no second chance.
9. William exclaimed, "So Ulla was a descendant of Asher!"
10. Hagar met an angel in the desert.

Hidden Cities

Underline the cities in the sentences below. The first city has been underlined.

1. One can achieve much in his life with Christ.
2. He refused to worship the bronze idol.
3. *The end* or *the last* are other words for omega.
4. Martha then said unto Jesus, "If thou hadst been here, my brother had not died."
5. Let Christ be the light of your life.
6. Sid once taught our Sunday-school class.
7. God gave man a superior intelligence, and so dominion was his.
8. Jack said, "An ephod was an emblem of the priestly office."
9. Honesty requires diligence.
10. Gil gallantly stands up for his beliefs.

Hidden Jewels and Metals

Underline the jewel or metal in the sentences below. The first one has been underlined.

1. Jim goes to a big, old church on Main Street.
2. Please try to keep Earl out of trouble.
3. Heaven is sometimes referred to as having a gate.
4. Esau had much hair on his arms.
5. God gave Moses a little admonition.
6. Jonathan, try to tame thy stiff temper.
7. Mike declared, "A cop performs useful services for citizens!"
8. We know that insanity was sometimes cured by Jesus.
9. Did anyone try to stop Azariah from encouraging Asa to destroy the idols in Judah?
10. Indeed, I am on doubtful terms with Suzanne.

Association—1

Associate each of the items below with these five headings. Place the number of each word or phrase beside the appropriate heading.

Creation

Noah and the Flood

The Ten Commandments

The Parables of Jesus

The Story of Pentecost

1. Moses
2. Shem
3. Adam
4. in the beginning
5. the sower
6. the rich fool
7. a rushing mighty wind
8. began to speak with other tongues
9. Mount Sinai
10. Mount Ararat
11. let there be light
12. cloven tongues like as of fire
13. the Prodigal Son
14. no other gods before me
15. the breath of life

Association—2

Associate each of the phrases below with these five headings. Place the number of each phrase beside the appropriate heading.

The Sower

The Good Samaritan

The Rich Fool

The Lost Sheep

The Prodigal Son

1. pull down my barns and build greater
2. ninety and nine
3. I am no more worthy to be called thy son
4. fell among thieves, which wounded him
5. take thine ease, eat, drink, and be merry
6. some fell among thorns
7. other fell into good ground
8. I have found my sheep which was lost
9. wasted his substance with riotous living
10. he passed by on the other side
11. my son was dead, and is alive again
12. some seeds fell by the way side
13. go after that which is lost, until he find it
14. brought him to an inn, and took care of him
15. hired servants of my father's have bread enough and to spare

Association—3

Associate each of the phrases below with these five headings. Place the number of each phrase beside the appropriate heading.

Lion

Hypocrite

Ahab

Water

Obedience

1. king of Israel
2. used in baptism
3. took possession of Naboth's vineyard
4. a promise to lengthen life
5. killed by David
6. holier than thou
7. professing but not practicing
8. used for the punishment of criminals
9. children to parents
10. dogs licked up his blood
11. Christ changed it to wine
12. married Jezebel and turned to idolatry
13. Samson's riddle
14. fierce beast
15. Jesus walked upon it

Association—4

Associate each of the phrases or words below with these five headings. Place the number of each phrase or word beside the appropriate heading.

Angels

Twelve

Idolatry

Sects

Altar

1. strictly forbidden
2. could be made of earth
3. sons of Jacob
4. Nazarenes
5. spiritual beings
6. Sadducees
7. an innumerable company
8. designed for sacrifice
9. prohibited by the first commandment
10. Herodians
11. neither marry, nor are given in marriage
12. ministered to Christ
13. Christ's disciples
14. Michael
15. tribes of Israel

Association—5

Associate each of the phrases or words below with these five headings. Place the number of each phrase or word beside the appropriate heading.

The Second Coming of Christ

Timothy

Lot

Serpent

Goat

1. cursed by God
2. of an unknown time
3. used for food
4. his father was a Greek
5. son of Haran
6. every eye shall see Him
7. shall eat dust
8. called the devil
9. Paul wrote to him
10. his wife looked back
11. hair used for clothing
12. wicked scoff at it
13. a companion of Paul
14. pitched his tent toward Sodom
15. rod of Moses

Women

These women of the Bible are found in the following word rectangle. The names are found horizontally, vertically, and diagonally. Some names are even spelled in reverse, and some letters are used more than once. Circle each name you find in the word rectangle.

Abi
Abigail
Adah
Anna
Deborah
Esther
Eve
Gomer
Hagar
Hannah
Herodias
Jael
Jezebel
Jochebed
Leah
Lois
Lydia
Martha
Mary
Miriam
Orpah
Priscilla
Rahab
Ruth
Sarah
Shua
Vashti
Zilpah
Zipporah

Z	O	A	B	I	G	A	I	L	U
Z	I	P	V	A	S	R	E	R	S
H	A	P	R	O	E	A	E	I	H
A	L	R	P	H	H	M	Z	A	U
R	B	I	T	O	O	Y	G	D	A
O	J	S	V	G	R	A	H	A	B
B	E	C	H	A	R	A	S	H	Z
E	A	I	M	O	V	M	H	L	D
D	H	L	O	O	I	A	E	V	E
L	T	L	B	R	N	A	R	A	B
O	R	A	I	N	J	I	O	S	E
I	A	A	A	G	A	D	D	H	H
S	M	H	T	U	R	Y	I	T	C
J	E	Z	E	B	E	L	A	I	O
H	H	A	P	L	I	Z	S	L	J

Animals

These animals from the Bible are found in the following word rectangle. The words are found horizontally, vertically, and diagonally. Some words are even spelled in reverse, and some letters are used more than once. Circle each animal you find in the word rectangle.

ant
ass
bat
bear
bees
camel
caterpillar
coney
cow
deer
dog
dove
fish
flies
fox
frog
goat
grasshopper
hart
hawk
horse
locusts
moth
mouse
mule
owl
ox
pelican
serpent
sheep
snail
swan
swine
weasel
whale

W	E	A	S	E	L	B	E	M	N	C
G	Y	E	N	O	C	B	A	O	A	A
O	R	S	E	R	P	E	N	T	C	M
A	X	A	X	L	U	A	E	H	I	E
T	S	X	S	H	U	R	F	E	L	L
S	O	S	E	S	P	M	R	S	E	A
F	L	W	I	I	H	G	O	U	P	H
N	S	L	L	F	D	O	G	O	H	W
E	W	L	F	E	A	L	P	M	D	P
S	A	Y	V	N	H	I	D	P	E	B
R	N	O	T	I	A	A	B	E	E	S
O	D	C	O	W	R	N	H	U	R	R
H	A	W	K	S	T	S	U	C	O	L

Places

These places from the Bible are found in the following word rectangle. The places are found horizontally, vertically, and diagonally. Some places are even spelled in reverse, and some letters are used more than once. Circle each place you find in the word rectangle.

Aphrah	Luz
Bethlehem	Lystra
Capernaum	Misgab
Dan	Myra
Eden	Neah
Ekron	Pai
Ephesus	Patmos
Golan	Philippi
Hai	Rome
Hebron	Shushan
Jezreel	Sidon
Joppa	Syracuse
Kanah	Tarsus
Kir	Zair
Lasha	Zaphon

A H S A L E E R Z E J I
S A H A I M D A N P P N
Y R U M O R P O Y P R O
R T S R E H R U I A I R
A S H M O K K L A T K B
C Y A N E R I A Z M A E
U L N O Z H G E I O N H
S S E E P H E S U S A B
E U D M G E G L I R H O
U S E O I A U D H U S M
O R L A B Z O P O T Y Y
C A P E R N A U M R E K
N T J O P P A H A E N B

Men

These men from the Bible are found in the following word rectangle. The names are found horizontally, vertically, and diagonally. Some names are even spelled in reverse, and some letters are used more than once. Circle each name you find in the word rectangle.

Aaron	David	Lot
Abimelech	Eli	Luke
Absalom	Enoch	Malachi
Adam	Esau	Mark
Ahaz	Ezra	Matthew
Ahi	Felix	Naaman
Amos	Gad	Nebuchadnezzar
Amram	Ham	Omri
Arad	Hezekiah	Pilate
Asa	Hur	Pul
Asher	Isaac	Samuel
Baal	Isaiah	Seth
Balaam	Jacob	Silas
Barnabas	James	Simon
Benjamin	Jeremiah	Terah
Boaz	Joel	Timothy
Cain	Joseph	Uriah
Cyrus	Lamech	Zur
Dan	Levi	

R	U	H	E	Z	E	K	I	A	H	I	I	E	B
A	M	R	A	M	L	L	E	U	M	A	S	M	A
Z	A	C	M	H	E	U	S	D	F	H	A	A	R
Z	T	H	U	A	V	P	E	I	E	A	I	L	N
E	T	C	M	I	I	O	T	V	L	Z	A	A	A
N	H	O	O	M	R	I	H	A	I	U	H	C	B
D	E	N	L	E	O	J	B	D	X	R	A	H	A
A	W	E	A	R	Z	E	E	I	N	O	M	I	S
H	M	S	S	E	N	G	S	U	R	Y	C	O	I
C	A	J	B	J	B	A	A	L	H	A	J	N	L
U	R	I	A	H	A	D	U	T	I	J	A	A	A
B	K	M	N	C	A	A	O	N	O	A	M	O	S
E	I	U	O	N	O	M	U	S	M	E	E	Z	H
N	D	A	R	A	I	B	E	A	C	K	S	A	E
P	I	L	A	T	E	P	N	H	U	O	Z	O	R
T	E	R	A	H	H	C	E	L	E	M	I	B	A

Parts of Man's Body

These parts of the body are found in the following word rectangle. The words are found horizontally, vertically, and diagonally. Some words are even spelled in reverse, and some letters are used more than once. Circle each word you find in the word rectangle.

ankle
arm
back
belly
cheek
chest
chin
ear
elbow
eye
finger
foot
hair
hand
head
heel
hip
jaw
knee
leg
lips
mouth
nail
neck
nose
nostril
shoulder
skin
stomach
thigh
thumb
toe
tongue

M	U	H	N	A	R	M	U	S	K	I	N
K	I	E	W	O	B	L	E	G	E	S	E
P	C	A	S	T	O	M	A	C	H	T	S
K	J	N	U	L	I	A	N	O	N	A	O
N	E	K	T	O	N	G	U	E	O	D	N
E	C	L	O	Y	L	L	E	B	S	N	O
E	H	E	J	M	D	F	O	O	T	A	D
B	E	Y	O	E	E	Y	E	N	R	H	A
M	S	U	R	E	G	N	I	F	I	A	E
U	T	O	H	G	I	H	T	S	L	E	H
H	H	E	E	L	C	S	P	A	A	J	U
T	O	T	O	E	T	I	K	R	I	A	H
E	K	C	A	B	L	C	H	E	E	K	O

Items From the Old Testament

These items from the Old Testament are found in the following word rectangle. The items are found horizontally, vertically, and diagonally. Some words are even spelled in reverse, and some letters are used more than once. Circle each word you find in the word rectangle.

angel
ark
birthright
bow
brick
cloud
coat
corn
covenant
day
evil

famine
flood
harp
iron
kindred
language
man
nation
pit
rain

rib
seed
son
sword
tent
token
tower
twins
vineyard
wife
wood

K O R W E N C P U D U O L C A E
U I O E E O O D I T U W E R T F
B B V K R O V R A T O U K A H I
R U O N I D E S F O M A N U G W
E T Y A E W N W D R A Y E N I V
N D A V O L A O A G T K C I R B
I O D T E A N R U N O P R A H E
M O S N I W T D E E V I L S T A
A L O D E C A T A N O R I O R N
F F E A O I K I N D R E D N I G
I E F A E G A U G N A L K A B E
S I T A N O I T A N A T R O E L

True or False—Part 1

Try to determine which of the statements below are true and which are false.

1. Samson carried away the gates of Gaza.
2. Saul was a choice young man.
3. Joseph had his father embalmed.
4. Moses saw the face of God.
5. The angel of the Lord appeared unto Manoah first and later to his wife.
6. Achan's punishment was hanging.
7. Daniel found favor with the prince of the eunuchs.
8. John the Baptist baptized Jesus.
9. Barabbas only committed robbery.
10. The fifth chapter of the Book of Malachi predicts the birth of Christ.
11. Nabal was a righteous man.
12. David generously rewarded the messenger who brought the news of Saul's death.
13. Christ's disciples were not given authority to cast out devils.
14. Dinah was the daughter of Jacob and Leah.
15. Jephthah offered his only daughter as a burnt offering to the Lord.

True or False—Part 2

Try to determine which of the statements below are true and which are false.

1. Dorcas was raised from the dead by Peter.
2. The great flood was sent as punishment for the great wickedness of man.
3. Only men could take the vow of a Nazarite.
4. There were cities of refuge for persons responsible for accidental manslaughter.
5. Michal praised David for leaping and dancing before the Lord.
6. Isaac was a poor man.
7. The chief priests and elders persuaded the multitude to ask for the release of Barabbas and not Jesus.
8. Melchizedek blessed Abraham.
9. The Israelites, fearing the increasing numbers of Egyptians, enslaved the Egyptians.
10. We deceive ourselves if we say that we have no sin.
11. Zacharias and Elisabeth were both righteous before God.
12. Peter converted and baptized the Ethiopian eunuch who held great authority under Queen Candace.
13. The multitude cried "Hosanna" to Jesus when He entered Jerusalem.
14. Paul was never imprisoned.
15. Elisha cast his mantle upon Elijah.

True or False—Part 3

Try to determine which of the statements below are true and which are false.

1. God gave directions to Moses for the construction of the ark of the covenant.
2. The Philistines, seeking revenge, attacked the Israelites after David slew Goliath.
3. Eli praised his righteous sons.
4. The last word in the Book of Revelation is *amen*.
5. Christ's twelve disciples were also called epistles.
6. Paul testified to the Jews that Jesus was Christ.
7. Cain never married.
8. The dogs licked up Ahab's blood.
9. Sergius Paulus, a wicked man, refused to hear the word of God from Barnabas and Paul.
10. Peter was never guilty of lying.
11. Christ was crucified alone on Golgotha.
12. Achan was killed in the valley of Achor.
13. Mephibosheth was the lame son of Jonathan.
14. Paul walked upon the water with Jesus.
15. Jesus sometimes spoke in parables.

True or False—Part 4

Try to determine which of the statements below are true and which are false.

1. The Lord sent Ananias to Saul of Tarsus after Saul's conversion.
2. Only Noah, his wife, and the animals were saved in the ark.
3. James wrote the Book of Revelation.
4. From Saul's shoulders and upward, he was higher than any of his people.
5. Achan sinned by working on the Sabbath.
6. Michal, Saul's daughter, loved David.
7. Gideon destroyed the altar and grove of Baal.
8. Rahab, her father's household, and all that she had were saved because she hid the messengers which Joshua had sent to spy out Jericho.
9. Jesus personally baptized a great multitude of people.
10. Pharaoh refused to allow Joseph's father and brothers to dwell in Goshen.
11. Jesus met the Samaritan woman at Jacob's well.
12. The Spirit of God descended like a dove when Jesus was baptized.
13. God prepared a gourd to shadow Jonah as he watched Nineveh.
14. Absalom was admired for his beauty.
15. Elimelech moved to Moab with Naomi, his wife, and his two sons.

Only One Is True—Part 1

Only one sentence from each group of five sentences is true. Pick out the true statement in each group.

1. Jacob first met Rachel at the market.
2. Bath-sheba appealed to David for Absalom as the successor to the throne.
3. King David built an altar at the threshing place of Araunah.
4. Miriam and Aaron never spoke against Moses, their brother.
5. Boaz was a beggar.

1. Esther wasn't a beautiful woman.
2. Adam lived longer than Noah.
3. Peter and John were educated men.
4. Leah stole her father's images.
5. Moses made a serpent of brass for the healing of the Israelites.

Only One Is True—Part 2

Only one sentence from each group of five sentences is true. Pick out the true statement in each group.

1. The breastplate of the high priests contained no precious stones.
2. The tip of the right ear of priests was anointed with water.
3. David rejoiced at the death of Saul.
4. A caravan of Israelites bought Joseph.
5. Joshua hung the king of Ai on a tree.

1. Tabitha did many good works.
2. Hannah had only one child.
3. Paul admonished Simon for trying to buy the power of the Holy Ghost.
4. The Book of Romans is an epistle of Peter.
5. None of Zipporah's sons were ever circumcised.

Only One Is True—Part 3

Only one sentence from each group of five sentences is true. Pick out the true statement in each group.

1. Saul never feared David.
2. Pilate washed his hands and proclaimed his innocence concerning Christ's crucifixion.
3. Job was a man of little substance.
4. Only animals with blemishes were used as offerings.
5. The people of Nineveh refused to turn from their evil ways after Jonah preached to them.

1. The Holy Ghost descended upon the apostles when the day of Pentecost was fully come.
2. Paul said that God was the author of confusion.
3. Lot was the son of Ishmael.
4. Amnon killed Absalom.
5. Solomon was the first to practice bigamy.

Only One Is False—Part 1

Only one sentence from each group of five sentences is false. Pick out the false statement in each group.

1. Ehud killed Eglon, king of Moab.
2. Athaliah was a wicked counselor to her son, King Ahaziah.
3. Crispus, the chief ruler of the synagogue, believed on the Lord.
4. Hanun shamed the servants which David had sent to comfort him after his father's death.
5. Samuel's sons were as righteous as their father.

1. After the flood, Noah planted a vineyard and became intoxicated.
2. Joseph never forgave his brothers.
3. Bar-jesus was a sorcerer, a false prophet, and a Jew.
4. Abishag, a young Shunammite woman, ministered to David in his old age.
5. The daughter of Herodias danced before Herod on his birthday.

Only One Is False—Part 2

Only one sentence from each group of five sentences is false. Pick out the false statement in each group.

1. The queen of Sheba, hearing of the fame of Solomon, visited him.
2. Anna was a prophetess.
3. David could play the harp well.
4. Samuel suggested to the elders of Israel that they choose a king to judge them.
5. Job had a daughter named Jemima.

1. Jesus first appeared unto Mary Magdalene and the other Mary after He arose.
2. Absalom polled the hair on his head every year.
3. Thomas expressed his disbelief when the other disciples told him that they had seen Christ after He had arisen.
4. The Holy Ghost revealed to Simeon, a devout man in Jerusalem, that he would see Christ before he died.
5. Reuben suggested to his brothers that they should not kill Joseph, but sell him.

Women

Unscramble the names of the women below.

1. vee ____________________
2. trhu ____________________
3. rasha ____________________
4. liedhal ____________________
5. yadil ____________________
6. kebhaer ____________________
7. ramy ____________________
8. roahbed ____________________
9. theesr ____________________
10. htebasile ____________________
11. zebejel ____________________
12. heal ____________________
13. nanahh ____________________
14. ramimi ____________________
15. hatarm ____________________

Animals

Unscramble the names of the animals below.

1. vedo ______
2. xfo ______
3. grof ______
4. sas ______
5. niwes ______
6. rath ______
7. ogd ______
8. agto ______
9. pehse ______
10. nilo ______
11. sebe ______
12. hifs ______
13. leic ______
14. pertsen ______
15. stolucs ______

Cities

Unscramble the names of the cities below.

1. more ______
2. popaj ______
3. sajemelur ______
4. morohagr ______
5. nad ______
6. theelb ______
7. yert ______
8. nerok ______
9. zeelejr ______
10. thezaran ______
11. pipipilh ______
12. creney ______
13. susehep ______
14. breonh ______
15. veenhin ______

Men

Unscramble the names of the men below.

1. pula ______________________
2. tanahn______________________
3. esfsut______________________
4. utsti ______________________
5. rhu______________________
6. sjseu ______________________
7. alamobs ______________________
8. enso______________________
9. anho ______________________
10. jdue ______________________
11. veil ______________________
12. toyimht ______________________
13. riuah ______________________
14. sheoa ______________________
15. caanh______________________

Plants

Unscramble the names of the plants below.

1. sagsr ______
2. fxal ______
3. illise ______
4. bruulhs ______
5. twahe ______
6. karamend ______
7. yoresocm ______
8. stillen ______
9. oonni ______
10. mapl ______
11. lockec ______
12. glirac ______
13. yelbra ______
14. sleke ______
15. dacre ______

Quotations—1

Try to determine the speaker of each quotation.

1. "It is finished."
2. "If ye had not plowed with my heifer, ye had not found out my riddle."
3. "Where is he that is born King of the Jews? for we have seen his star in the east, and are come to worship him."
4. "Verily I say unto thee, To day shalt thou be with me in paradise."
5. "The serpent beguiled me, and I did eat."
6. "Who is on the Lord's side? let him come unto me."
7. "Behold, I will put a fleece of wool in the floor; and if the dew be on the fleece only, and it be dry upon all the earth beside, then shall I know that thou wilt save Israel by mine hand, as thou hast said."
8. "For dust thou art, and unto dust shalt thou return."
9. "Sun, stand thou still upon Gibeon; and thou, Moon, in the valley of Ajalon."
10. "Go and wash in Jordan seven times, and thy flesh shall come again to thee, and thou shalt be clean."

Quotations—2

Try to determine the speaker of each quotation.

1. "Father, into thy hands I commend my spirit."
2. "With the jawbone of an ass, heaps upon heaps, with the jaw of an ass have I slain a thousand men."
3. "And I will take away mine hand, and thou shalt see my back parts: but my face shall not be seen."
4. "This is now bone of my bones, and flesh of my flesh."
5. "And it shall be, when he lieth down, that thou shalt mark the place where he shall lie, and thou shalt go in, and uncover his feet, and lay thee down; and he will tell thee what thou shalt do."
6. "Thus saith the Lord, Set thine house in order; for thou shalt die, and not live."
7. "Whosoever hath any gold, let them break it off. So they gave it me: then I cast it into the fire, and there came out this calf."
8. "Come, let us make our father drink wine, and we will lie with him, that we may preserve seed of our father."
9. "Think not that I am come to destroy the law, or the prophets: I am not come to destroy, but to fulfil."
10. "Lord, I am not worthy that thou shouldest come under my roof: but speak the word only, and my servant shall be healed."

Quotations—3

Try to determine the speaker of each quotation.

1. "Thou canst not see my face: for there shall no man see me, and live."
2. "Thou dost but hate me, and lovest me not: thou hast put forth a riddle unto the children of my people, and hast not told it me."
3. "My punishment is greater than I can bear."
4. "I thirst."
5. "And let them judge the people at all seasons: and it shall be, that every great matter they shall bring unto thee, but every small matter they shall judge: so shall it be easier for thyself, and they shall bear the burden with thee."
6. "They that be whole need not a physician, but they that are sick."
7. "Give me here John Baptist's head in a charger."
8. "Peradventure there be fifty righteous within the city: wilt thou also destroy and not spare the place for the fifty righteous that are therein?"
9. "Dost thou now govern the kingdom of Israel? arise, and eat bread, and let thine heart be merry: I will give thee the vineyard of Naboth the Jezreelite."
10. "Whomsoever I shall kiss, that same is he: hold him fast."

Quotations—4

Try to determine the speaker of each quotation.

1. "And fear not them which kill the body, but are not able to kill the soul: but rather fear him which is able to destroy both soul and body in hell."
2. "I have sinned in that I have betrayed the innocent blood."
3. "Is it true, O Shadrach, Meshach, and Abednego, do not ye serve my gods, nor worship the golden image which I have set up?"
4. "My God hath sent his angel, and hath shut the lions' mouths, that they have not hurt me."
5. "And go quickly, and tell his disciples that he is risen from the dead; and, behold, he goeth before you into Galilee; there shall ye see him: lo, I have told you."
6. "I will serve thee seven years for Rachel thy younger daughter."
7. "Master, it is good for us to be here: and let us make three tabernacles; one for thee, and one for Moses, and one for Elias."
8. "If thou hadst been here, my brother had not died."
9. "Shall I go and call to thee a nurse of the Hebrew women, that she may nurse the child for thee?"
10. "Why was not this ointment sold for three hundred pence, and given to the poor?"

Quotations—5

Try to determine the speaker of each quotation.

1. "Suffer the little children to come unto me, and forbid them not: for of such is the kingdom of God."
2. "Master, behold, the fig tree which thou cursedst is withered away."
3. "Hast thou considered my servant Job, that there is none like him in the earth, a perfect and an upright man, one that feareth God, and escheweth evil?"
4. "Would to God we had died by the hand of the Lord in the land of Egypt, when we sat by the flesh pots, and when we did eat bread to the full; for ye have brought us forth into this wilderness, to kill this whole assembly with hunger."
5. "The voice is Jacob's voice, but the hands are the hands of Esau."
6. "Truly this man was the Son of God."
7. "I stand in the presence of God; and am sent to speak unto thee, and to shew thee these glad tidings."
8. "Glory to God in the highest, and on earth peace, good will toward men."
9. "Somebody hath touched me: for I perceive that virtue is gone out of me."
10. "How is it that thou, being a Jew, askest drink of me, which am a woman of Samaria?"

Quotations—6

Try to determine the speaker of each quotation.

1. "If it be so, our God whom we serve is able to deliver us from the burning fiery furnace, and he will deliver us out of thine hand, O king."
2. "Thy name shall be called no more Jacob, but Israel: for as a prince hast thou power with God and with men, and hast prevailed."
3. "Lord, by this time he stinketh: for he hath been dead four days."
4. "What is this dream that thou hast dreamed? Shall I and thy mother and thy brethren indeed come to bow down ourselves to thee to the earth?"
5. "Hosanna: Blessed is the King of Israel that cometh in the name of the Lord."
6. "If ye shall ask any thing in my name, I will do it."
7. "I find in him no fault at all."
8. "Except I shall see in his hands the print of the nails, and put my finger into the print of the nails, and thrust my hand into his side, I will not believe."
9. "Silver and gold have I none; but such as I have give I thee: In the name of Jesus Christ of Nazareth rise up and walk."
10. "Is it lawful for a man to put away his wife?"

Quotations—7

Try to determine the speaker of each quotation.

1. "Grant unto us that we may sit, one on thy right hand, and the other on thy left hand, in thy glory."
2. "We have sinned, for we have spoken against the Lord, and against thee; pray unto the Lord, that he take away the serpents from us."
3. "Verily I say unto you, That this poor widow hath cast more in, than all they which have cast into the treasury."
4. "Lord, now lettest thou thy servant depart in peace, according to thy word: For mine eyes have seen thy salvation."
5. "Ananias, why hath Satan filled thine heart to lie to the Holy Ghost, and to keep back part of the price of the land?"
6. "Lord, lay not this sin to their charge."
7. "I heard thy voice in the garden, and I was afraid, because I was naked; and I hid myself."
8. "Go to, let us go down, and there confound their language, that they may not understand one another's speech."
9. "Thy money perish with thee, because thou hast thought that the gift of God may be purchased with money."
10. "Saul, Saul, why persecutest thou me?"

Matching—1

Place the correct letter in each blank.

1. God loveth a cheerful ______.
2. Andrew brought Simon Peter to ______.
3. Paul preached at Mars' ______.
4. Samson slew ______ men at Ashkelon.
5. Lazarus was a ______.
6. Simon was compelled to carry the ______.
7. David smote Goliath's ______.
8. Asa was ______ of Judah.
9. ______ begged for the body of Jesus.
10. David once hid in a ______.
11. Be ye ______ and multiply.
12. Mordecai was a ______.
13. They shall lay hands on the ______.
14. A priest was supposed to burn ______.
15. Bitter ______ were eaten during the Passover.

A. beggar
B. forehead
C. Joseph
D. herbs
E. cave
F. Jesus
G. incense
H. Jew
I. sick
J. thirty
K. fruitful
L. cross
M. giver
N. king
O. hill

Matching—2

Place the correct letter in each blank.

1. Barns were used for the storing of ______.
2. Noah became a ______ after the flood.
3. David became Saul's ______.
4. Gomer was the wife of ______.
5. The snail was considered an ______ animal.
6. Great ______ of people followed Christ.
7. Ishmael dwelt in the wilderness and became an ______.
8. From his roof, David saw Bath-sheba ______.
9. Esau was born red all over like a ______ garment.
10. Husband and wife shall be one ______.
11. Consider the ______ of the field.
12. With His finger, Jesus wrote on the ______.
13. The earth is God's ______.
14. Elijah wore a ______.
15. The Lord set a ______ upon Cain.

A. footstool
B. multitudes
C. mark
D. Hosea
E. mantle
F. flesh
G. unclean
H. lilies
I. husbandman
J. hairy
K. ground
L. archer
M. seed
N. bathing
O. armourbearer

Matching—3

Place the correct letter in each blank.

1. Herod had James killed with the ______.
2. Jehoram had an incurable ______.
3. Pashur put Jeremiah in the ______.
4. Rahab was a ______.
5. Lapidoth was the husband of ______.
6. There was an ______ at Christ's death.
7. Timothy's mother was ______.
8. Rahab hid the two spies among the stalks of ______.
9. Daniel had a vision of four great ______.
10. Joseph's brothers conspired against him to ______ him.
11. Nabal refused to give food to ______.
12. Jezrahiah was an overseer of ______.
13. The ______ cast lots for Christ's vesture.
14. ______ was the champion Philistine of Gath.
15. Joab fetched a ______ woman of Tekoah.

A. soldiers
B. wise
C. disease
D. flax
E. singers
F. beasts
G. sword
H. Goliath
I. David
J. Deborah
K. slay
L. harlot
M. Eunice
N. earthquake
O. stocks

Matching—4

Place the correct letter in each blank.

1. Jesus is evidence of God's ______.
2. The Lord descended upon Mount Sinai in ______.
3. Jesse's three eldest sons joined Saul's ______.
4. Set thine ______ in order: for thou shalt die.
5. Jacob was a plain man, dwelling in ______.
6. Take heed lest any man ______ you.
7. From the beginning of the creation God made them male and ______.
8. Judas committed ______.
9. Count it all joy when ye fall into divers ______.
10. The day of the Lord will come as a ______ in the night.
11. Regard not them that have familiar ______.
12. No ______ could come upon the head of a Nazarite.
13. Saul became David's ______.
14. Jesus washed His disciples' ______.
15. A crown of ______ was placed upon Christ's head.

A. house
B. thorns
C. thief
D. enemy
E. love
F. temptations
G. deceive
H. razor
I. army
J. feet
K. fire
L. female
M. tents
N. suicide
O. spirits

Matching—5

Place the correct letter in each blank.

1. Hell is described as a lake of ______.
2. He that loveth not knoweth not ______.
3. John the Baptist baptized with ______ unto repentance.
4. Michal let David down through a ______ to provide David's escape.
5. ______ be the name of God for ever and ever.
6. My kingdom is not of this ______.
7. The children of Israel went to Deborah for ______.
8. Joseph of Arimathaea went to Pilate and begged for the ______ of Christ.
9. He kept him as the ______ of his eye.
10. Moses married an ______ woman.
11. Naboth was carried out of the city and ______.
12. Now we see through a ______, darkly.
13. King Eglon was a very ______ man.
14. The ______ gave up the dead which were in it.
15. Annas sent Jesus, his bound prisoner, to ______.

A. blessed
B. world
C. body
D. glass
E. fat
F. Ethiopian
G. fire
H. Caiaphas
I. stoned
J. window
K. sea
L. God
M. judgment
N. apple
O. water

Matching—6

Place the correct letter in each blank.

1. Adullam was a ______.
2. Pashur smote ______.
3. Jesus is the bread of ______.
4. Candace was queen of ______.
5. The swine was an ______ animal.
6. Jacob wrestled with an angel at ______.
7. Prepare to meet thy God, O ______.
8. Eglon was king of ______.
9. Samson died with the ______.
10. Samuel's firstborn was ______.
11. Saul cast a ______ at David.
12. Elijah called down fire from ______.
13. Shamgar slew six hundred Philistines with an ox ______.
14. Job was smitten with ______.
15. The ______ always ye have with you.

A. Ethiopia	I. unclean
B. Moab	J. javelin
C. Joel	K. cave
D. Jeremiah	L. Philistines
E. heaven	M. Israel
F. poor	N. Peniel
G. goad	O. life
H. boils	

Word Additions—Men
Part 1

A man's name will result when the proper words are added in each sentence.

1. Add a stair tread to a female chicken, and get a Christian martyr. (*Answer:* step + hen = Stephen.)
2. Add a pronoun for a male person to a straight stick, and get a wicked king.
3. Add the fifteenth letter of the English alphabet to a piece of furniture for sleeping on, and get an ancestor of Jesus.
4. Add the sixteenth letter of the Greek alphabet to tardy, and get a governor of Judea.
5. Add stockings to an indefinite article used before words beginning with the consonant sound, and get one of the minor prophets.
6. Add nay to an exclamation of delight, and get a true survivor.
7. Add a musical piece to be performed by one person to the abbreviation for the second day of the week, and get a child of David.
8. Add an indefinite article used before words beginning with a vowel sound to sketched, and get a disciple of Christ.
9. Add the first letter of the English alphabet to the barrier to stop flowing water, and get an early man.
10. Add the tall, spare man who personifies the United States to a male offspring, and get a strong man.

Word Additions—Men
Part 2

A man's name will result when the proper words are added in each sentence.

1. Add an exclamation of greeting to a male sheep, and get a king who built a house for David.
2. Add a flat piece of material which covers a floor to muscle, and get a publican who became a disciple.
3. Add an exclamation of triumph to an adult male person, and get the person who was hanged on the gallows which he had prepared for Mordecai.
4. Add the twenty-first letter of the Greek alphabet to one of the fleshy folds forming the edges of the mouth, and get one of the twelve apostles.
5. Add a very small amount to the upper hind leg of a hog, and get a son of Jerubbaal.
6. Add a quick blow to the opposite of out, and get a king of Hazor.
7. Add a tamed animal which is treated fondly to a suffix forming the comparative degree, and get a disciple who denied Jesus.
8. Add a family of snakes that kill their prey by constriction or pressure to the last letter of the English alphabet, and get an ancestor of Christ.
9. Add the present tense of *be* which is used with I to a male sheep, and get the father of a deliverer.
10. Add the twenty-first letter of the Greek alphabet to a small, sour, pale yellow citrus fruit, and get a Christian to whom Paul addressed one of his epistles.

Word Additions—Places

A place name will result when the proper words are added in each sentence.

1. Add the fifth letter of the English alphabet to the lair of a wild animal, and get a place which had a beautiful garden.
2. Add the preposition for on or near to female chickens, and get a Grecian city where Paul taught.
3. Add the tall, spare man who personifies the United States to a melody especially for solo voice, and get a city built and named by King Omri.
4. Add the metal container in which liquids and foods are sealed for preservation to an indefinite article used before words beginning with the consonant sound, and get the city where Jesus performed His first miracle.
5. Add the black liquid from wood or coal to a generic name for a pig, and get the birthplace of a famous missionary.
6. Add the twenty-first letter of the Greek alphabet to one of the fleshy folds forming the edges of the mouth to the sixteenth letter of the Greek alphabet, and get a city of Macedonia where Paul was persecuted.
7. Add a slang word for a girl to a pronoun for oneself to the side away from the wind, and get the area which was the scene of most of Christ's life.
8. Add a pronoun for a female person to mother, and get a city of Judah.
9. Add angry to the opposite of off, and get a Canaanite city.
10. Add the last letter of the English alphabet to a pole with a flat blade for rowing, and get an ancient city of the land of Canaan.

Symbols

Underline the correct term which corresponds to each symbol below.

1. crimson—holiness, iniquity, obedience
2. Magog—children of God, enemies of God, love
3. white—purity, sin, sorrow
4. dove—shame, Satan, Holy Ghost
5. helmet—patience, innocence, salvation
6. lamp—the Word of God, Pharisees, scorn
7. girdle—wrath, truth, evil
8. cross—redemption, war, food
9. dragon—wisdom, security, Satan
10. shield—riches, faith, poverty

Unfamiliar Names

Below is a list of ten relatively unfamiliar names of biblical characters. Circle the familiar name for each character from each group.

1. Israel—Ishmael, Enoch, Jacob
2. Edom—Saul, Esau, Dan
3. Belteshazzar—Boaz, Ahab, Daniel
4. Jonas—Jonah, Jeremiah, Jonathan
5. Oshea—Ezra, Joshua, Aaron
6. Hadassah—Priscilla, Esther, Lydia
7. Mara—Naomi, Martha, Jezebel
8. Reuel—Reuben, Jesus, Jethro
9. Mishael—Noah, Meshach, Titus
10. Azariah—Abednego, Zacharias, Adam

Double Letters—Men

Using the clues given below, try to complete the men's names.

1. A a _ _ _ a priest
2. _ _ _ _ b b _ _ a robber
3. _ _ c c _ _ _ _ _ a publican
4. _ _ _ d d _ _ _ _ a disciple of Christ
5. _ _ _ _ _ e e the father of two of Christ's disciples
6. _ _ g g _ _ a prophet mentioned in the Book of Ezra
7. _ _ _ _ k k _ _ a prophet and poet after the destruction of Nineveh
8. _ _ _ _ p p _ the king who heard the appeal of Festus for Paul
9. _ s s _ _ _ _ _ the fifth son of Leah
10. _ _ t t _ _ _ a disciple of Christ

Double Letters—Women and Men

Using the clues below, try to complete the men and women's names below.

1. _ _ a a _ the father of twins
2. _ a a _ _ _ a Syrian general healed of leprosy
3. _ _ l l _ _ Lamech's wife who gave birth to Tubalcain
4. _ _ _ _ _ _ _ l l _ the wife of Aquila
5. _ n n _ a prophetess
6. _ _ n n _ _ a woman who gave her son back to God
7. _ _ p p _ _ _ _ a woman who fell dead after she lied before Peter
8. _ _ p p _ _ _ _ a woman who circumcised her own son
9. _ _ _ _ _ _ _ z z _ _ the Babylonian king slain during an impious feast
10. _ _ _ _ _ _ _ _ _ _ _ z z _ _ a powerful Babylonian king

Diagonal Letters—1

Using the clues below, try to complete the puzzle.

1. A h _ _
2. _ a h _ _
3. _ _ a h
4. _ _ _ a h
5. _ _ _ _ a h
6. _ _ _ _ _ a h
7. _ _ _ _ _ _ a h
8. _ _ _ _ _ _ _ a h
9. _ _ _ _ _ _ _ _ a h

1. He took possession of Naboth's vineyard.
2. She was a harlot of Jericho, who hid the Hebrew spies.
3. He was the father of Shem, Ham, and Japheth.
4. This disobedient prophet was the son of Amittai.
5. This Tishbite was the prophet who predicted a great drought.
6. She asked Samson to disclose the secret of his strength.
7. Isaiah told this king to set his house in order because he was going to die. Isaiah returned to tell this king that the Lord had decided to heal him.
8. He was a minor prophet as well as an adviser of King Uzziah.
9. He was the son of Enoch.

Diagonal Letters—2

Using the clues below, try to complete the puzzle.

1. T h _ _ _ _
2. _ t h _ _ _ _ _
3. _ _ t h
4. _ _ _ t h _ _ _ _ _ _
5. _ _ _ _ t h _ _
6. _ _ _ _ _ t h
7. _ _ _ _ _ _ t h
8. _ _ _ _ _ _ _ t h
9. _ _ _ _ _ _ _ _ t h

1. He was one of the twelve disciples of Christ.
2. She, the mother of King Ahaziah, seized the throne when her son died.
3. He was a son of Adam and Eve.
4. He was one of Christ's twelve apostles.
5. David took care of this man's lame son.
6. He entered into the ark of Noah.
7. He was the son of Uriah the priest.
8. King Solomon worshiped this goddess of the Zidonians.
9. He, a son of Saul, reigned over Israel for two years.

Bible Match—1

Three or more people can play this game. A designated player reads aloud these incomplete phrases and sentences, and each player secretly completes them by writing one or more words on a blank sheet of paper. Each player successively reveals his response when everyone has finished. Each player with a matching response receives one point, and play continues in this manner. At the end of the game the player with the greatest number of points wins the game.

1. Solomon's ______ (wisdom, wives, wealth, and so forth)
2. ______ was a disciple of Christ. (Matthew, Peter, and so forth)
3. Mount ______
4. ______ was a large city.
5. the ______ Sea
6. the ark of ______
7. the ______ of life
8. the valley of ______
9. During the crucifixion, Christ said ______ .
10. ______ was a fisherman.
11. the parable of the ______
12. the garden of ______
13. Moses ______ Canaan.
14. Christ healed the ______.
15. I am the ______.

Bible Match—2

Three or more people can play this game. A designated player reads aloud these incomplete phrases and sentences, and each player secretly completes them by writing one or more words on a blank sheet of paper. Each player successively reveals his response when everyone has finished. Each player with a matching response receives one point, and play continues in this manner. At the end of the game the player with the greatest number of points wins the game.

1. _____ is another name for the Israelites.
2. _____ is a musical instrument mentioned in the Bible.
3. Wood was sometimes used for _____ .
4. _____ was stoned.
5. _____ lived in Egypt.
6. Prayer is _____ .
7. _____ came to worship the baby Jesus.
8. The Bible is _____ .
9. _____ was a wicked city.
10. Oil was used for _____ .
11. _____ displayed jealousy.
12. _____ slew many Philistines.
13. Another name for God is _____ .
14. Genesis tells the story of _____ .
15. _____ was a tax collector.

Bible Match—3

Three or more people can play this game. A designated player reads aloud these incomplete phrases and sentences, and each player secretly completes them by writing one or more words on a blank sheet of paper. Each player successively reveals his response when everyone has finished. Each player with a matching response receives one point, and play continues in this manner. At the end of the game the player with the greatest number of points wins the game.

1. _____ committed murder.
2. _____ was an article of clothing.
3. _____ was considered a clean animal.
4. Jonathan and _____
5. _____ was taken into captivity.
6. _____ had more than one wife.
7. The Bible mentions that _____ fasted for several days.
8. Strife can be caused by _____ .
9. _____ was a prophet.
10. God told Adam to _____ .
11. _____ followed Christ.
12. Paul preached _____ .
13. _____ experienced a famine.
14. _____ is a disease mentioned in the Bible.
15. _____ was a judge.

Bible Match—4

Three or more people can play this game. A designated player reads aloud these incomplete phrases and sentences, and each player secretly completes them by writing one or more words on a blank sheet of paper. Each player successively reveals his response when everyone has finished. Each player with a matching response receives one point, and play continues in this manner. At the end of the game the player with the greatest number of points wins the game.

1. Jesus performed a miracle at ______ .
2. Gold was used for ______ .
3. Christ cared for ______ .
4. Elijah was ______ .
5. ______ was one of the duties of a wife.
6. ______ loved David.
7. The desert was ______ .
8. ______ was filled with the Holy Ghost.
9. God changed the name of ______ .
10. ______ was barren.
11. the Holy ______
12. The wise men presented ______ to the baby Jesus.
13. Houses were built of ______ .
14. ______ was a wealthy man.
15. the wilderness of ______

Bible Match—5

Three or more people can play this game. A designated player reads aloud these incomplete phrases and sentences, and each player secretly completes them by writing one or more words on a blank sheet of paper. Each player successively reveals his response when everyone has finished. Each player with a matching response receives one point, and play continues in this manner. At the end of the game the player with the greatest number of points wins the game.

1. There are many ______ in heaven.
2. ______ was anointed by Samuel.
3. ______ was sometimes used to make jewelry.
4. Salvation is by ______ .
5. ______ was hanged.
6. ______ was a Nazarite.
7. ______ was one of the duties of the priests.
8. ______ was obedient to God.
9. ______ was cast into prison.
10. ______ was a hunter.
11. One mode of punishment was ______ .
12. Another name for the Bible is ______ .
13. Manna was ______ .
14. Pride can lead to ______ .
15. ______ was a good mother.

Bible Match—6

Three or more people can play this game. A designated player reads aloud these incomplete phrases and sentences, and each player secretly completes them by writing one or more words on a blank sheet of paper. Each player successively reveals his response when everyone has finished. Each player with a matching response receives one point, and play continues in this manner. At the end of the game the player with the greatest number of points wins the game.

1. ______ is another name for Jerusalem.
2. ______ committed suicide.
3. Christ ______ the multitude.
4. ______ was a Pharisee.
5. Blessed are the ______ .
6. The kingdom of heaven is likened to ______ .
7. One type of offering was a ______ .
8. A lamb is symbolic of ______ .
9. One of Isaiah's prophecies was about ______ .
10. ______ rebelled against God.
11. ______ had long hair.
12. ______ was made of stone.
13. ______ was saved by Christ.
14. ______ was a wicked woman.
15. ______ rode an ass.

Find Other Words

This is a game for two or more players. Select a word from the Bible and make other words from the letters it contains. Each player secretly writes his words on a blank sheet of paper. These words must consist of two or more letters, and no plurals are allowed. The time limit can be set at five minutes (or longer). The player who finds the greatest number of words is the winner.

A variation can occur by playing the game orally. In this case, the players take turns finding different words. Each player who cannot find a new word must drop out of the game, and play continues in this manner until one player, the winner, remains.

Example—sacrifice

as	face
fire	rise
care	if
fear	and so forth

Alphabet Game

This is an oral game for two or more players. The first player names a biblical character whose name begins with the letter A, and the second player names a biblical character whose name begins with the letter B. Play continues in this manner through the entire alphabet, and the play may continue through the entire alphabet more than once before a winner is determined. A player must drop out of the game if he cannot name a character whose name begins with the specified letter, and that same letter is passed on to the next player. A certain letter is omitted if no player is able to name a character whose name begins with that letter, and the play resumes as before. Names cannot be duplicated. Play continues until one player, the winner, remains.

A variation can occur by substituting different subjects, such as biblical cities and animals, for the biblical characters.

Memory Game

This is a game for two or more players. The players choose a biblical category such as places of the Bible. A designated player writes the list of places as the other players name them at random. The list may comprise thirty or more places, according to the discretion of the players. One player quickly reads the complete list aloud, and the list is then covered. Each player tries to secretly list as many of the places as he can remember. Each player reveals his list at the end of ten minutes, and the player with the longest list wins the game.

Fill in the Columns

This is a game for two or more players. Each player secretly fills in columns for a set time limit of five minutes (or longer). A biblical category, such as men of the Bible, is selected, and one name, such as Belshazzar, is chosen as the starting word. The players proceed to fill in different men's names beneath each letter of the starting word. No names can be duplicated, and only one name can be used per column. Since each player receives one point for each letter he uses in each name, the players who fill in longer names receive more points. The player with the greatest number of points wins the game.

Example

	B	E	L	S	H	A	Z	Z	A	R		
1	a	l	a	a	a	h	a		d	e		
2	r	i	z	m	r	a	c		a	h		
3	t	m	a	u	a	b	c		m	o		
4	i	e	r	e	n		h			b		
5	m	l	u	l			a			o		
6	a	e	s				e			a		
7	e	c					u			m		
8	u	h					s					
9	s											
10												
11												
12												
13												

Bartimaeus	9 points
Elimelech	8 points
Lazarus	6 points
Samuel	5 points
Haran	4 points
Ahab	3 points
Zacchaeus	8 points
Z	0 points
Adam	3 points
Rehoboam	7 points
Total	53 points

Bible Pantomime

This is a game for three or more players. Each player secretly thinks of biblical scenes which he would like to pantomime. One player is selected at random to start the game. This starting player acts his scene while the other players try to guess it. The player who correctly guesses the scene exchanges places with the starting player. If no one can correctly guess the scene being pantomimed, then the "actor" tells his scene and proceeds to pantomime another scene. Play continues in this manner until the players decide to end the game. David slaying Goliath, Christ's crucifixion, and Peter walking upon the water are some scenes which can be pantomimed.

A variation can occur by the division of players into teams, and each team tries to stump the other team.

Answers

Riddles—1

1. Nebuchadnezzar (Daniel 4:33)
2. Jonah or Jonas (Matthew 12:40)
3. Adam and Eve (Genesis 3:1–19)
4. Moses (Exodus 17:10–12)
5. Peter (Matthew 17:24–27)
6. Sapphira (Acts 5:1–10)
7. Naomi (Ruth 1:1–18)
8. The servant who received one talent in the parable of the talents (Matthew 25:14–18).
9. Lot (Genesis 19:26)
10. Cain didn't raise sheep because he wasn't Abel.

Riddles—2

1. John the Baptist (Matthew 14:3–11)
2. Job (Job 1:1)
3. Adam (Genesis 2)
4. The witch of En-dor (1 Samuel 28:7–14)
5. The Book of Exodus tells how Pharaoh's daughter drew Moses out of water (Exodus 2:5–10).
6. Zacharias (Luke 1:13–22)
7. Samson (Judges 15:4, 5)
8. Moses (Exodus 32:19)
9. The Holy Ghost
10. The poor widow (Mark 12:42–44)

Riddles—3

1. Adam's fall
2. Nebuchadnezzar (Daniel 2:25–33)
3. David (1 Samuel 16:11–13; 2 Samuel 2:11)
4. The ladder of Jacob's vision (Genesis 28:10–12)
5. Goliath (1 Samuel 17)
6. Saul who was later called Paul (Acts 9:1–6)
7. Unleavened bread
8. Absalom (2 Samuel 18:9, 10)
9. Stephen (Acts 6:1–8; Acts 7:58–60)
10. Pilate

Riddles—4

1. Joseph (Genesis 41:39–45)
2. Jesus or Peter (Matthew 14:25–29)
3. Solomon (1 Kings 4:23)
4. Joseph (Genesis 37:25–28)
5. The woman with an alabaster box of ointment of spikenard (Mark 14:3)
6. Lazarus (John 11:38–44)
7. Jacob (Genesis 37:33, 34)
8. Naaman (2 Kings 5:9–14)
9. Adam (Genesis 3:7)
10. Mephibosheth, a lame man (2 Samuel 9:6–13)

Riddles—5

1. Solomon (1 Kings 3:5–12)
2. Pharaoh's horses drew chariots.
3. Lazarus the beggar (Luke 16:20, 21)
4. The Bible
5. Balaam (Numbers 22:28–30)
6. Noah's ark (Genesis 6:13–22)
7. Adam (Genesis 2:21, 22)
8. The woman who had an issue of blood for twelve years (Matthew 9:20, 21)
9. The Book of Ephesians begins with Paul addressing the people.
10. Eve (Genesis 4:1)

Hidden Women

1. Asa, Raham, and Ezbon are men who can be found in the Bible.
2. Sin can mar your testimony.
3. Adam walked thru the garden.
4. The veil was worn by women for concealment.
5. Belshazzar indulged in a great feast while a hand wrote upon the wall.
6. Can you tell me in which era Chelubai lived?
7. Pride can mar that inner communion with God.
8. Ah, a garden is a lovely place in which to pray.
9. How many places thereabouts did Paul visit?
10. Other than Nahum, were there any prophets of Judah?

Hidden Men

1. He finally learned to set hate aside.
2. Melissa ultimately asked for forgiveness.
3. Kate said, "I will watch my step henceforth."
4. Even tho' *master* had various meanings, Christ was addressed as "Master."
5. Jessica invited me to church next Sunday.
6. Ann finally accepted Christ as her Saviour.
7. God can deliver us from all evil.
8. I know that he's austere in his beliefs.
9. A Christian is also known as a believer.
10. Jan said, "Papa ultimately became a preacher."

Hidden Diseases

1. She thought that the Pharisees were a little prosy.
2. Usually a pal sympathizes with you.
3. They used a unit of dry measure known as cab.
4. He said, "I know about salvation; it changes your life."
5. Wicked kings sometimes staged foul ceremonies.
6. Abraham always displayed courtesy to a guest.
7. The rods of Moses and Aaron were supreme rods.
8. The Jews would not drop symbolism from their religious heritage.
9. The old man said, "Rub oil slowly into your wounds."
10. If every Christian would work harder, more people would be saved.

Hidden Numbers

1. The first woman was Eve.
2. Mother spoke of our dedication.
3. I am going to the rummage sale today, but Pat went yesterday.
4. The preacher's sermon was on eternal life.
5. Herodias, Eve, Naomi, and Leah were all mothers.
6. The old woman ate not of the fig tree.
7. Marsha asked, "If I verify your story, will you help me?"
8. Jim laughed, "You should have seen Bob's face when Beth reeled in that huge trout!"
9. Rachel, Eve, Naamah, and Miriam can all be found in the Old Testament.
10. Genesis records the curse of Cain in exile.

Hidden Books of the Bible

1. The old woman screamed, "Tim, O, thy healing was a miracle!"
2. Thebez, Rama, and Penuel are cities that can be found in the Bible.
3. An encampment of the Israelites near Mount Hor was called a Mosera.
4. Faith can wipe terror from one's brow.
5. Martha keeps alms for the poor.
6. She said, "I am at the Women's Bible League Meeting."
7. One can study the tact so wonderfully exemplified by Jesus.
8. Terry shouted, "The answer is Ai. Aha, it's the city near the site of Abraham's first altar!"
9. Jud gestures frequently when he talks about Christ.
10. I have my Bible with me, but Gene's is in our car.

Hidden Parts of Man

1. Be ye therefore as little children.
2. They, Sarah and Rebekah, were barren until God blessed them.
3. Anna, I like to study the Book of Genesis.
4. Abraham left his kin and moved away.
5. Did Paul ever go to Ephesus?
6. Humbly, she admitted her mistake.
7. We are in charge of organizing the new committee.
8. Sometimes there is no second chance.
9. William exclaimed, "So Ulla was a descendant of Asher!"
10. Hagar met an angel in the desert.

Hidden Cities

1. One can achieve much in his life with Christ.
2. He refused to worship the bronze idol.
3. *The end* or *the last* are other words for omega.
4. Martha then said unto Jesus, "If thou hadst been here, my brother had not died."
5. Let Christ be the light of your life.
6. Sid once taught our Sunday-school class.
7. God gave man a superior intelligence, and so dominion was his.
8. Jack said, "An ephod was an emblem of the priestly office."
9. Honesty requires diligence.
10. Gil gallantly stands up for his beliefs.

Hidden Jewels and Metals

1. Jim goes to a big, old church on Main Street.
2. Please try to keep Earl out of trouble.
3. Heaven is sometimes referred to as having a gate.
4. Esau had much hair on his arms.
5. God gave Moses a little admonition.
6. Jonathan, try to tame thy stiff temper.
7. Mike declared, "A cop performs useful services for citizens!"
8. We know that insanity was sometimes cured by Jesus.
9. Did anyone try to stop Azariah from encouraging Asa to destroy the idols in Judah?
10. Indeed, I am on doubtful terms with Suzanne.

Association—1

Creation—3, 4, 11, 15
Noah and the Flood—2, 10
The Ten Commandments—1, 9, 14
The Parables of Jesus—5, 6, 13
The Story of Pentecost—7, 8, 12

1. (Exodus 20)
2. (Genesis 7:13)
3. (Genesis 1, 2)
4. (Genesis 1:1)
5. (Matthew 13:1–9)
6. (Luke 12:16–21)
7. (Acts 2:1, 2)
8. (Acts 2:4)
9. (Exodus 19, 20)
10. (Genesis 8:4)
11. (Genesis 1:3)
12. (Acts 2:3)
13. (Luke 15:11–32)
14. (Exodus 20:3)
15. (Genesis 2:7)

Association—2

The Sower—6, 7, 12
The Good Samaritan—4, 10, 14
The Rich Fool—1, 5
The Lost Sheep—2, 8, 13
The Prodigal Son—3, 9, 11, 15

1. (Luke 12:18)
2. (Luke 15:4)
3. (Luke 15:21)
4. (Luke 10:30)
5. (Luke 12:19)
6. (Matthew 13:7)
7. (Matthew 13:8)
8. (Luke 15:6)
9. (Luke 15:13)
10. (Luke 10:31)
11. (Luke 15:24)
12. (Matthew 13:4)
13. (Luke 15:4)
14. (Luke 10:34)
15. (Luke 15:17)

Association—3

Lion—5, 8, 13, 14
Hypocrite—6, 7
Ahab—1, 3, 10, 12
Water—2, 11, 15
Obedience—4, 9

1. (1 Kings 16:29)
2. (Matthew 3:11)
3. (1 Kings 21:16)
4. (Ephesians 6:1–3)
5. (1 Samuel 17:34–36)
6. (Isaiah 65:5)
7. (Matthew 23:3, 4)
8. (Daniel 6:16)
9. (Ephesians 6:1)
10. (1 Kings 22:37–40)
11. (John 2:2–9)
12. (1 Kings 16:30, 31)
13. (Judges 14:12–18)
14. (Job 4:10)
15. (Matthew 14:25)

Association—4

Angels—5, 7, 11, 12, 14
Twelve—3, 13, 15
Idolatry—1,9
Sects—4, 6, 10
Altar—2, 8

1. (Exodus 20:4)
2. (Exodus 20:24)
3. (Genesis 35:22–26)
4. (Acts 24:5)
5. (Hebrews 1:13, 14)
6. (Acts 5:17)
7. (Hebrews 12:22)
8. (Exodus 20:24)
9. (Exodus 20:3)
10. (Matthew 22:16)
11. (Matthew 22:30)
12. (Luke 22:43)
13. (Matthew 10:1–4)
14. (Revelation 12:7)
15. (Genesis 49:28)

Association—5

The Second Coming of Christ—2, 6, 12
Timothy—4, 9, 13
Lot—5, 10, 14
Serpent—1, 7, 8, 15
Goat—3, 11

1. (Genesis 3:14)
2. (Matthew 24:36)
3. (Genesis 27:9)
4. (Acts 16:1)
5. (Genesis 11:27)
6. (Revelation 1:7)
7. (Genesis 3:14)
8. (Revelation 12:9)
9. (1 Timothy 1:1, 2)
10. (Genesis 19:26)
11. (Numbers 31:20)
12. (2 Peter 3:3, 4)
13. (Acts 16:1–4)
14. (Genesis 13:12)
15. (Exodus 4:1–3)

Women

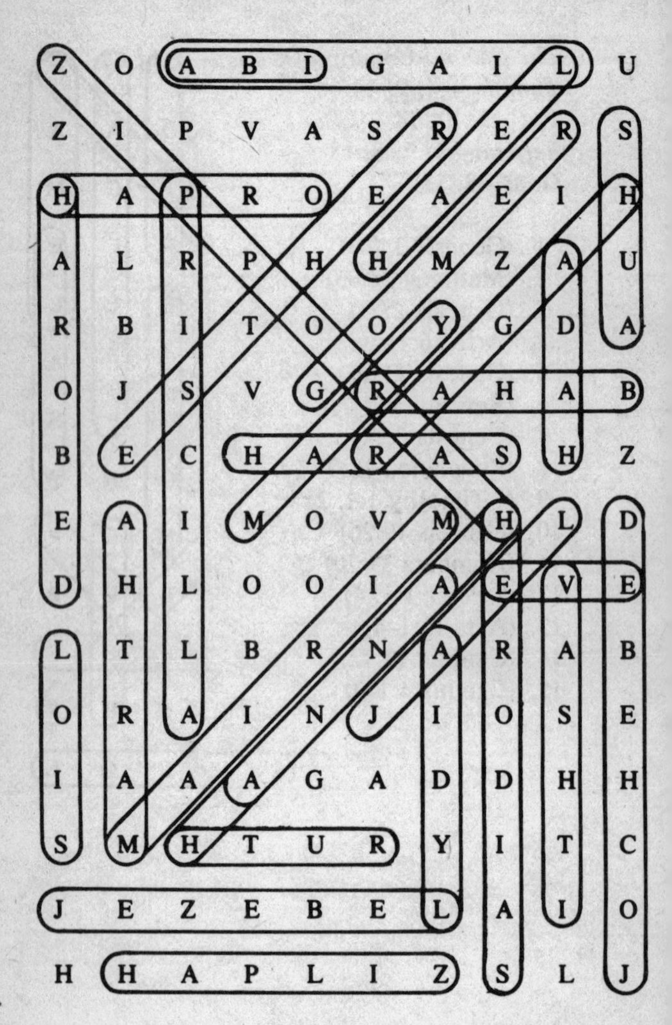
Z O A B I G A I L U
Z I P V A S R E R S
H A P R O E A E I H
A L R P H H M Z A U
R B I T O O Y G D A
O J S V G R A H A B
B E C H A R A S H Z
E A I M O V M H L D
D H L O O I A E V E
L T L B R N A R A B
O R A I N J I O S E
I A A A G A D D H H
S M H T U R Y I T C
J E Z E B E L A I O
H H A P L I Z S L J

Animals

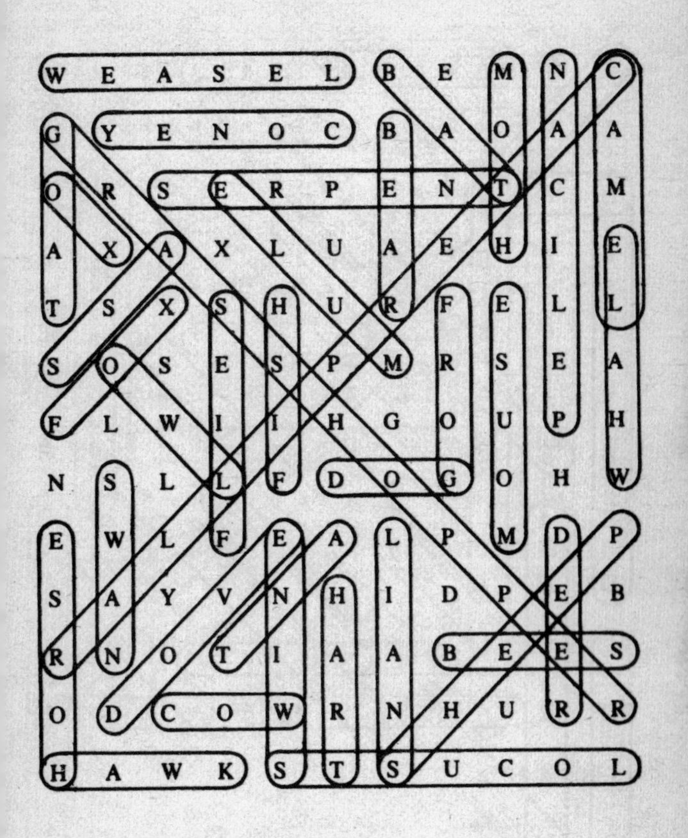
W E A S E L B E M N C
G Y E N O C B A O A A
O R S E R P E N T C M
A X A X L U A E H I E
T S X S H U R F E L L
S O S E S P M R S E A
F L W I I H G O U P H
N S L L F D O G O H W
E W L F E A L P M D P
S A Y V N H I D P E B
R N O T I A A B E E S
O D C O W R N H U R R
H A W K S T S U C O L

Places

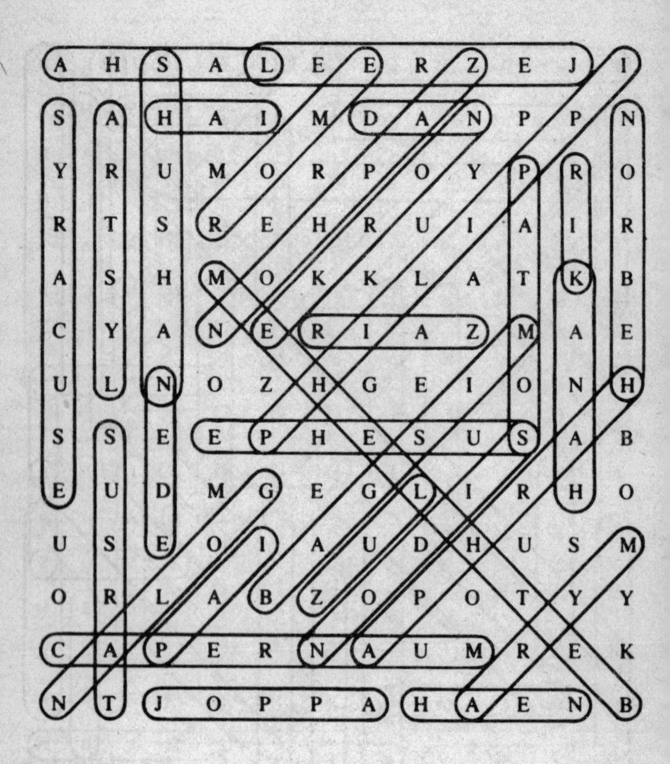
A H S A L E E R Z E J I
S A H A I M D A N P P N
Y R U M O R P O Y P R O
R T S R E H R U I A I R
A S H M O K K L A T K B
C Y A N E R I A Z M A E
U L N O Z H G E I O N H
S S E E P H E S U S A B
E U D M G E G L I R H O
U S E O I A U D H U S M
O R L A B Z O P O T Y Y
C A P E R N A U M R E K
N T J O P P A H A E N B

Men

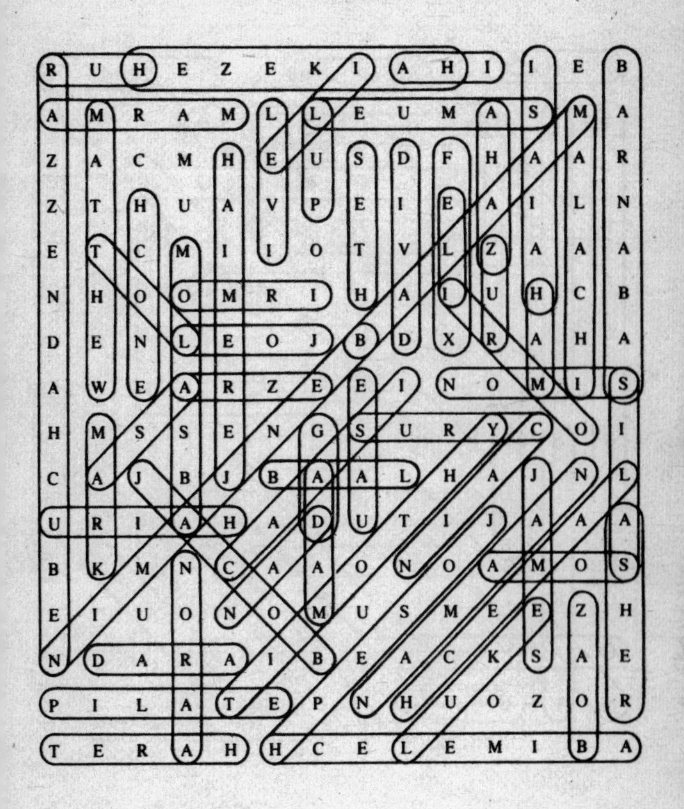

Parts of Man's Body

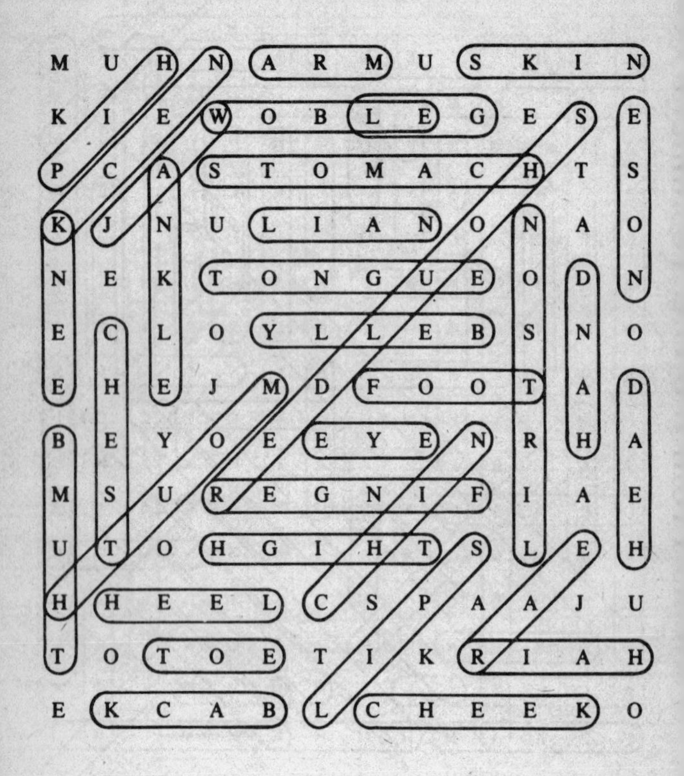

Items From the Old Testament

K	O	R	W	E	N	C	P	U	D	U	O	L	C	A	E
U	I	O	E	E	O	O	D	I	T	U	W	E	R	T	F
B	B	V	K	R	O	V	R	A	T	O	U	K	A	H	I
R	U	O	N	I	D	E	S	F	O	M	A	N	U	G	W
E	T	Y	A	E	W	N	W	D	R	A	Y	E	N	I	V
N	D	A	V	O	L	A	O	A	G	T	K	C	I	R	B
I	O	D	T	E	A	N	R	U	N	O	P	R	A	H	E
M	O	S	N	I	W	T	D	E	E	V	I	L	S	T	A
A	L	O	D	E	C	A	T	A	N	O	R	I	O	R	N
F	F	E	A	O	I	K	I	N	D	R	E	D	N	I	G
I	E	F	A	E	G	A	U	G	N	A	L	K	A	B	E
S	I	T	A	N	O	I	T	A	N	A	T	R	O	E	L

True or False—Part 1

1. True (Judges 16:1–3)
2. True (1 Samuel 9:2)
3. True (Genesis 50:2)
4. False (Exodus 33:20)
5. False (Judges 13:2–21)
6. False (Joshua 7:20–25)
7. True (Daniel 1:9)
8. True (Matthew 3:13–17)
9. False (Mark 15:7)
10. False (There are only four chapters in the Book of Malachi.)
11. False (1 Samuel 25:3)
12. False (2 Samuel 1:1–16)
13. False (Luke 9:1)
14. True (Genesis 30:19–21)
15. True (Judges 11:30–40)

True or False—Part 2

1. True (Acts 9:36–42)
2. True (Genesis 6:5–17)
3. False (Numbers 6:2)
4. True (Numbers 35:11, 12)
5. False (2 Samuel 6:16–23)
6. False (Genesis 26:12–14)
7. True (Matthew 27:20)
8. True (Genesis 14:18, 19)
9. False (Exodus 1:7–14)
10. True (1 John 1:8)
11. True (Luke 1:5, 6)
12. False (Acts 8:26–39)
13. True (Matthew 21:9–11)
14. False (Acts 16:19–23)
15. False (1 Kings 19:19)

True or False—Part 3

1. True (Exodus 25:10–21)
2. False (1 Samuel 17:51–53)
3. False (1 Samuel 2:22–25)
4. True (Revelation 22:21)
5. False (Matthew 10:1, 2)
6. True (Acts 18:5)
7. False (Genesis 4:17)
8. True (1 Kings 22:38–40)
9. False (Acts 13:7)
10. False (Mark 14:66–72)
11. False (Matthew 27:33–38)
12. True (Joshua 7:24–26)
13. True (2 Samuel 4:4)
14. False (Matthew 14:28, 29)
15. True (Matthew 13:1–3)

True or False—Part 4

1. True (Acts 9:10–18)
2. False (Genesis 7:7–10)
3. False (Revelation 1:1, 2)
4. True (1 Samuel 9:2)
5. False (Joshua 7:20–25)
6. True (1 Samuel 18:28)
7. True (Judges 6:25–27)
8. True (Joshua 6:25)
9. False (John 4:1, 2)
10. False (Genesis 47:5, 6)
11. True (John 4:5–7)
12. True (Matthew 3:16)
13. True (Jonah 4:5, 6)
14. True (2 Samuel 14:25)
15. True (Ruth 1:1, 2)

Only One Is True—Part 1

1. False (Genesis 29:1–12)
2. False (1 Kings 1:15–21)
3. True (2 Samuel 24:18–25)
4. False (Numbers 12:1)
5. False (Ruth 2:1)

1. False (Esther 2:7)
2. False (Genesis 5:5; Genesis 9:29)
3. False (Acts 4:13)
4. False (Genesis 31:19)
5. True (Numbers 21:8, 9)

Only One Is True—Part 2

1. False (Exodus 28:15–20)
2. False (Exodus 29:20)
3. False (2 Samuel 1:11, 12)
4. False (Genesis 37:28)
5. True (Joshua 8:28, 29)

1. True (Acts 9:36)
2. False (1 Samuel 2:21)
3. False (Acts 8:18–24)
4. False (Romans 1:1–7)
5. False (Exodus 4:25)

Only One Is True—Part 3

1. False (1 Samuel 18:29)
2. True (Matthew 27:24)
3. False (Job 1:1–3)
4. False (Leviticus 1:2, 3)
5. False (Jonah 3)

1. True (Acts 2:1–4)
2. False (1 Corinthians 14:33)
3. False (Genesis 11:27)
4. False (2 Samuel 18:14, 15)
5. False (Genesis 4:19)

Only One Is False—Part 1

1. True (Judges 3:14–25)
2. True (2 Chronicles 22:1–3)
3. True (Acts 18:8)
4. True (2 Samuel 10:1–5)
5. False (1 Samuel 8:1–3)

1. True (Genesis 9:20, 21)
2. False (Genesis 50:15–21)
3. True (Acts 13:6)
4. True (1 Kings 1:1–4)
5. True (Matthew 14:6)

Only One Is False—Part 2

1. True (2 Chronicles 9:1)
2. True (Luke 2:36)
3. True (1 Samuel 16:16–19)
4. False (1 Samuel 8:4–20)
5. True (Job 42:13, 14)

1. True (Matthew 28:1–10)
2. True (2 Samuel 14:25, 26)
3. True (John 20:24, 25)
4. True (Luke 2:25, 26)
5. False (Genesis 37:26, 27)

Women

1. Eve
2. Ruth
3. Sarah
4. Delilah
5. Lydia
6. Rebekah
7. Mary
8. Deborah
9. Esther
10. Elisabeth
11. Jezebel
12. Leah
13. Hannah
14. Miriam
15. Martha

Animals

1. dove
2. fox
3. frog
4. ass
5. swine
6. hart
7. dog
8. goat
9. sheep
10. lion
11. bees
12. fish
13. lice
14. serpent
15. locusts

Cities

1. Rome
2. Joppa
3. Jerusalem
4. Gomorrah
5. Dan
6. Bethel
7. Tyre
8. Ekron
9. Jezreel
10. Nazareth
11. Philippi
12. Cyrene
13. Ephesus
14. Hebron
15. Nineveh

Men

1. Paul
2. Nathan
3. Festus
4. Titus
5. Hur
6. Jesus
7. Absalom
8. Enos
9. Noah
10. Jude
11. Levi
12. Timothy
13. Uriah
14. Hosea
15. Achan

Plants

1. grass
2. flax
3. lilies
4. bulrush
5. wheat
6. mandrake
7. sycomore
8. lentils
9. onion
10. palm
11. cockle
12. garlic
13. barley
14. leeks
15. cedar

Quotations—1

1. Jesus (John 19:30)
2. Samson (Judges 14:18)
3. The wise men from the East (Matthew 2:2)
4. Jesus (Luke 23:43)
5. Eve (Genesis 3:13)
6. Moses (Exodus 32:26)
7. Gideon (Judges 6:37)
8. God (Genesis 3:19)
9. Joshua (Joshua 10:12)
10. Elisha (2 Kings 5:10)

Quotations—2

1. Jesus (Luke 23:46)
2. Samson (Judges 15:16)
3. God (Exodus 33:23)
4. Adam (Genesis 2:23)
5. Naomi (Ruth 3:4)
6. Isaiah (2 Kings 20:1)
7. Aaron (Exodus 32:24)
8. Lot's older daughter (Genesis 19:32)
9. Jesus (Matthew 5:17)
10. The centurion (Matthew 8:8)

Quotations—3

1. God (Exodus 33:20)
2. Samson's wife (Judges 14:16)
3. Cain (Genesis 4:13)
4. Jesus (John 19:28)
5. Jethro (Exodus 18:22)
6. Jesus (Matthew 9:12)
7. The daughter of Herodias (Matthew 14:8)
8. Abraham (Genesis 18:24)
9. Jezebel (1 Kings 21:7)
10. Judas (Matthew 26:48)

Quotations—4

1. Jesus (Matthew 10:28)
2. Judas (Matthew 27:4)
3. Nebuchadnezzar (Daniel 3:14)
4. Daniel (Daniel 6:22)
5. The angel speaking to Mary Magdalene and the other Mary (Matthew 28:7)
6. Jacob (Genesis 29:18)
7. Peter (Mark 9:5)
8. Martha (John 11:21) and Mary (John 11:32)
9. Miriam (Exodus 2:7)
10. Judas (John 12:5)

Quotations—5

1. Jesus (Mark 10:14)
2. Peter (Mark 11:21)
3. The Lord (Job 1:8)
4. The children of Israel (Exodus 16:3)
5. Isaac (Genesis 27:22)
6. The centurion (Mark 15:39)
7. The angel called Gabriel (Luke 1:19)
8. A multitude of the heavenly host (Luke 2:14)
9. Jesus (Luke 8:46)
10. The Samaritan woman at the well (John 4:9)

Quotations—6

1. Shadrach, Meshach, and Abednego (Daniel 3:17)
2. The angel which wrestled with Jacob (Genesis 32:28)
3. Martha (John 11:39)
4. Jacob (Genesis 37:10)
5. The people of Jerusalem (John 12:13)
6. Jesus (John 14:14)
7. Pilate (John 18:38)
8. Thomas (John 20:25)
9. Peter (Acts 3:6)
10. Pharisees (Mark 10:2)

Quotations—7

1. James and John (Mark 10:37)
2. The Israelites (Numbers 21:7)
3. Jesus (Mark 12:43)
4. Simeon (Luke 2:29, 30)
5. Peter (Acts 5:3)
6. Stephen (Acts 7:60)
7. Adam (Genesis 3:10)
8. The Lord (Genesis 11:7)
9. Peter (Acts 8:20)
10. The Lord (Acts 9:4)

Matching—1

1. M (2 Corinthians 9:7)
2. F (John 1:40–42)
3. O (Acts 17:22)
4. J (Judges 14:19)
5. A (Luke 16:20)
6. L (Matthew 27:32)
7. B (1 Samuel 17:49)
8. N (1 Kings 15:9)
9. C (Matthew 27:57, 58)
10. E (1 Samuel 22:1)
11. K (Genesis 9:7)
12. H (Esther 2:5)
13. I (Mark 16:18)
14. G (Luke 1:9)
15. D (Exodus 12:8)

Matching—2

1. M (Job 39:12)
2. I (Genesis 9:20)
3. O (1 Samuel 16:21)
4. D (Hosea 1:3)
5. G (Leviticus 11:29, 30)
6. B (Matthew 4:25)
7. L (Genesis 21:20)
8. N (2 Samuel 11:2, 3)
9. J (Genesis 25:25)
10. F (Matthew 19:5)
11. H (Matthew 6:28)
12. K (John 8:6)
13. A (Matthew 5:35)
14. E (2 Kings 2:8)
15. C (Genesis 4:15)

Matching—3

1. G (Acts 12:1, 2)
2. C (2 Chronicles 21:16–18)
3. O (Jeremiah 20:2)
4. L (Joshua 6:25)
5. J (Judges 4:4)
6. N (Matthew 27:50, 51)
7. M (2 Timothy 1:5)
8. D (Joshua 2:6)
9. F (Daniel 7)
10. K (Genesis 37:18)
11. I (1 Samuel 25:2–12)
12. E (Nehemiah 12:42)
13. A (John 19:23, 24)
14. H (1 Samuel 17:23)
15. B (2 Samuel 14:2)

Matching—4

1. E (1 John 4:9, 10)
2. K (Exodus 19:18)
3. I (1 Samuel 17:13)
4. A (Isaiah 38:1)
5. M (Genesis 25:27)
6. G (Mark 13:5)
7. L (Mark 10:6)
8. N (Matthew 27:3–5)
9. F (James 1:2)
10. C (2 Peter 3:10)
11. O (Leviticus 19:31)
12. H (Numbers 6:5)
13. D (1 Samuel 18:29)
14. J (John 13:5)
15. B (Matthew 27:29)

Matching—5

1. G (Revelation 20:15)
2. L (1 John 4:8)
3. O (Matthew 3:11)
4. J (1 Samuel 19:12)
5. A (Daniel 2:20)
6. B (John 18:36)
7. M (Judges 4:4, 5)
8. C (Matthew 27:57, 58)
9. N (Deuteronomy 32:10)
10. F (Numbers 12:1)
11. I (1 Kings 21:13)
12. D (1 Corinthians 13:12)
13. E (Judges 3:17)
14. K (Revelation 20:13)
15. H (John 18:24)

Matching—6

1. K (1 Samuel 22:1)
2. D (Jeremiah 20:2)
3. O (John 6:35)
4. A (Acts 8:27)
5. I (Deuteronomy 14:8)
6. N (Genesis 32:24–31)
7. M (Amos 4:12)
8. B (Judges 3:12)
9. L (Judges 16:30)
10. C (1 Samuel 8:2)
11. J (1 Samuel 18:11)
12. E (2 Kings 1:10)
13. G (Judges 3:31)
14. H (Job 2:7)
15. F (John 12:8)

Word Additions—Men Part 1

1. Stephen (step–hen)
2. Herod (he–rod)
3. Obed (o–bed)
4. Pilate (pi–late)
5. Hosea (hose–a)
6. Noah (no–ah)
7. Solomon (solo–Mon.)
8. Andrew (an–drew)
9. Adam (a–dam)
10. Samson (Uncle Sam–son)

Word Additions—Men Part 2

1. Hiram (hi–ram)
2. Matthew (mat–thew)
3. Haman (ha–man)
4. Philip (phi–lip)
5. Jotham (jot–ham)
6. Jabin (jab–in)
7. Peter (pet–er)
8. Boaz (boa–z)
9. Amram (am–ram)
10. Philemon (phi–lemon)

Word Additions—Places

1. Eden (e–den)
2. Athens (at–hens)
3. Samaria (Uncle Sam–aria)
4. Cana (can–a)
5. Tarsus (tar–sus)
6. Philippi (phi–lip–pi)
7. Galilee (gal–I–lee)
8. Shema (she–ma)
9. Madon (mad–on)
10. Zoar (z–oar)

Symbols

1. crimson—iniquity (Isaiah 1:18)
2. Magog—enemies of God (Revelation 20:7–9)
3. white—purity (Isaiah 1:18)
4. dove—Holy Ghost (John 1:32)
5. helmet—salvation (Ephesians 6:17)
6. lamp—the Word of God (Psalms 119:105)
7. girdle—truth (Ephesians 6:14)
8. cross—redemption (Colossians 2:13, 14)
9. dragon—Satan (Revelation 12:9)
10. shield—faith (Ephesians 6:16)

Unfamiliar Names

1. Israel—Jacob (Genesis 32:28)
2. Edom—Esau (Genesis 36:1)
3. Belteshazzar—Daniel (Daniel 1:7)
4. Jonas—Jonah (Jonah 1:17; Matthew 12:40)
5. Oshea—Joshua (Exodus 33:11; Numbers 13:16)
6. Hadassah—Esther (Esther 2:7)
7. Mara—Naomi (Ruth 1:20)
8. Reuel—Jethro (Exodus 2:16–21; Exodus 3:1)
9. Mishael—Meshach (Daniel 1:7)
10. Azariah—Abednego (Daniel 1:7)

Double Letters—Men

1. Aaron (Numbers 18:1)
2. Barabbas (John 18:40)
3. Zacchaeus (Luke 19:2)
4. Thaddaeus (Mark 3:14–18)
5. Zebedee (Mark 3:14–17)
6. Haggai (Ezra 5:1)
7. Habakkuk (the Book of Habakkuk)
8. Agrippa (Acts 25:13–21)
9. Issachar (Genesis 30:17, 18)
10. Matthew (Mark 3:14–18)

Double Letters—Women and Men

1. Isaac (Genesis 25:21–26)
2. Naaman (2 Kings 5:1–14)
3. Zillah (Genesis 4:19–22)
4. Priscilla (Acts 18:2)
5. Anna (Luke 2:36)
6. Hannah (1 Samuel 1:22–28)
7. Sapphira (Acts 5:1–10)
8. Zipporah (Exodus 4:25)
9. Belshazzar (Daniel 5:1–30)
10. Nebuchadnezzar (Daniel 1:1)

Diagonal Letters—1

1. Ahab (1 Kings 21:16)
2. Rahab (Joshua 2:1–4)
3. Noah (Genesis 5:32)
4. Jonah (Jonah 1:1–3)
5. Elijah (1 Kings 17:1)
6. Delilah (Judges 16:6)
7. Hezekiah (2 Kings 20:1–5)
8. Zechariah (2 Chronicles 26:1–5)
9. Methuselah (Genesis 5:21)

Diagonal Letters—2

1. Thomas (Matthew 10:1–3)
2. Athaliah (2 Chronicles 22:10–12)
3. Seth (Genesis 4:25)
4. Bartholomew (Matthew 10:1–3)
5. Jonathan (2 Samuel 9:6–13)
6. Japheth (Genesis 7:13)
7. Meremoth (Ezra 8:33)
8. Ashtoreth (1 Kings 11:4, 5)
9. Ish-bosheth (2 Samuel 2:10)